SEAL IN THE BATHTUB

by Paul L. Sieswerda
and Joy S. Reidenberg

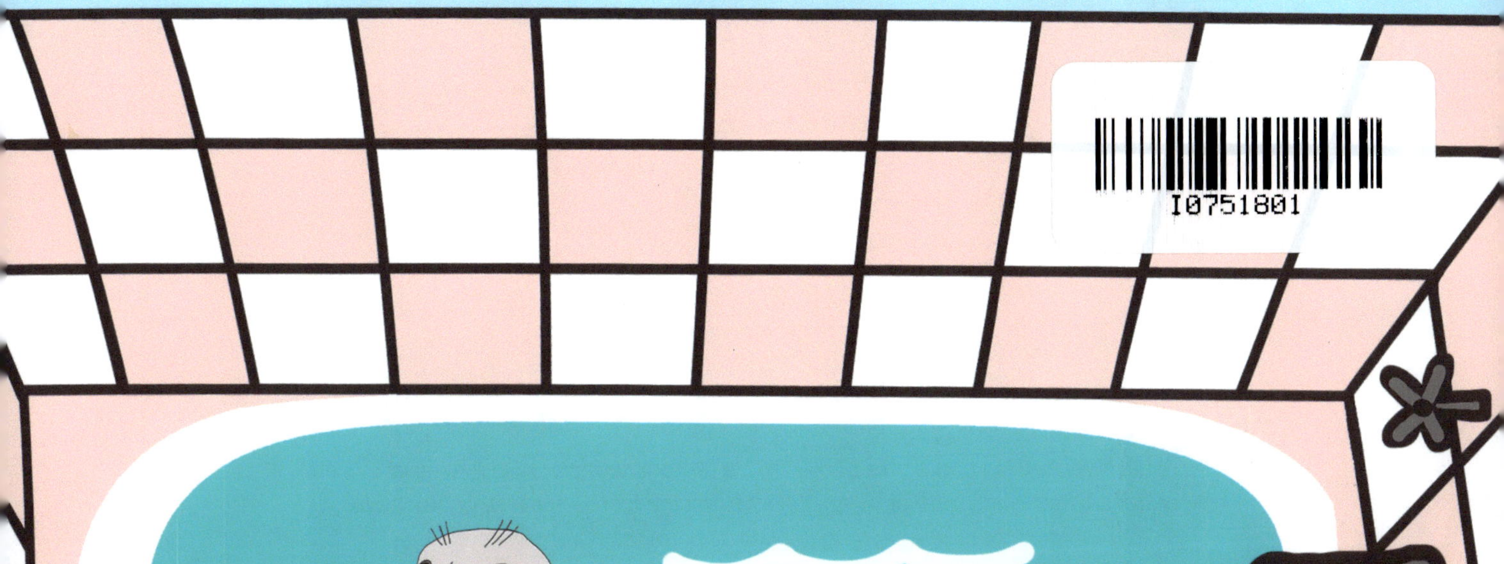

Illustrated by Joy S. Reidenberg

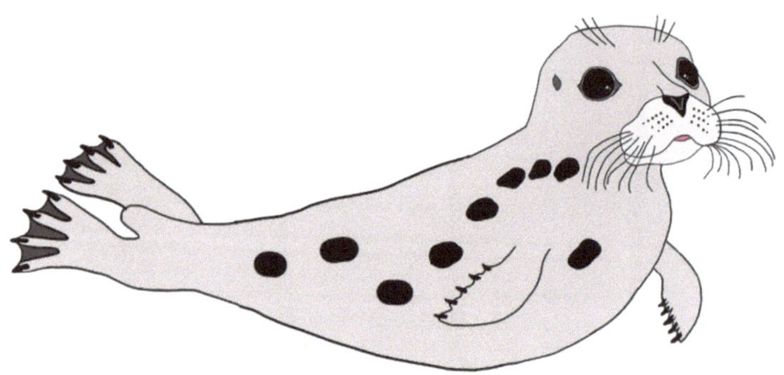

Best Publishing Company 631 US Highway 1, Suite 307 North Palm Beach, FL 33408

Photography: Paul L. Sieswerda, PJ Sieswerda, and Joy S. Reidenberg
Cover & Illustrations: Joy S. Reidenberg, PhD
Editing: Lorraine Fico White & Elizabeth Peterson
Layout: Lorie DeWorken

Library of Congress Control Number: 2025951352
ISBN: 978-0-941332-45-3 (paperback)
ISBN: 978-1-930536-55-5 (e Book)

Printed in USA

DEDICATION

For my father Paul L. Sieswerda, also known as “The Whale Man of New York City,” whose love for the ocean, passion for discovery, and quiet strength have inspired generations, starting with me.

Your stories, kindness, and curiosity have shaped not just me but my own sons, too. Three generations still look out to the water . . . all because of you. Thank you for showing me how to look closely, stay curious, listen deeply, and always follow the current, wherever it leads.

With endless love and admiration . . .
Your son,

PJ

Paul L. Sieswerda and Dorothy “Candi” Sieswerda in 2014, during an interview where they tell the story of Cecil.

Listen to the interview at:
Snap Judgment: Cecil The Seal
(soundcloud.com)

Photo of Cecil in the bathtub in 1978 at the Sieswerda family home in Massachusetts.

PREFACE

Seal in the Bathtub is a true story based on the experience of the late first author Paul Sieswerda, who wrote most of this story but died before the book was published.

Paul really did rehabilitate a baby seal at his private home while he was employed at the New England Aquarium in Boston, MA. His wife, Candi, and two young sons, Paul Jr. and Jeffrey, were eager to be involved in its care.

Today it is illegal to keep and care for a rescued baby seal or any other marine mammal at home. However, this story took place before there were such regulations. There were no coordinated national rescue efforts for stranded marine mammals.

Beached seals and other marine animals (such as sea lions, sea otters, manatees, dolphins, whales, and sea turtles) were handled by local volunteers and organizations with limited resources and no standardized rescue protocols. There was no centralized system for documenting, reporting, or analyzing strandings and no procedure established for data collection.

Today, NOAA* Fisheries' Marine Mammal Health and Stranding Response Program coordinates emergency responses to sick, injured, distressed, entangled, or dead marine mammals. Research conducted under their supervision advances scientific knowledge, is used in education programs, and supports conservation efforts.

* National Oceanic and Atmospheric Administration

Baby seals wash up on
the shore after a big storm.

An aquarium rescue team picks up the baby seals from the beach.

So many seals
are rescued!

The team brings the baby
seals to the aquarium.

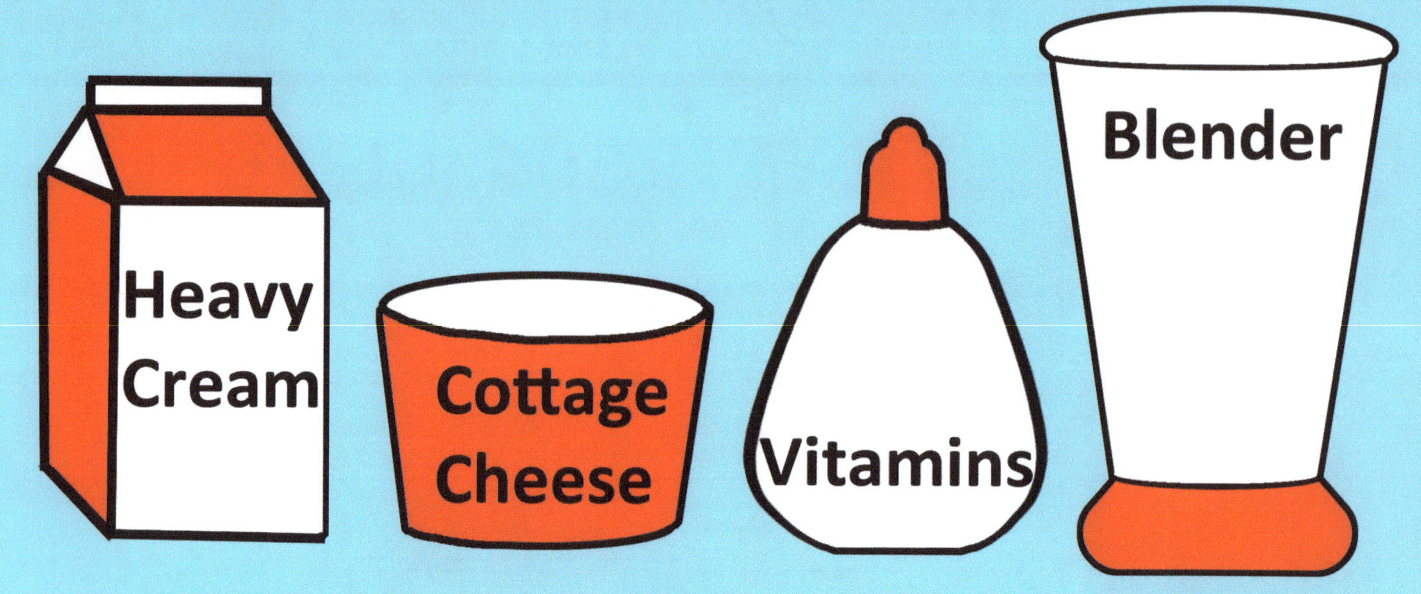

They use a recipe to make seal milk,

Yummy!

just like mother's rich milk.

Five baby bottles with seal milk.

One bottle for each feeding.
Five feedings every day.

Making the milk is so much work!

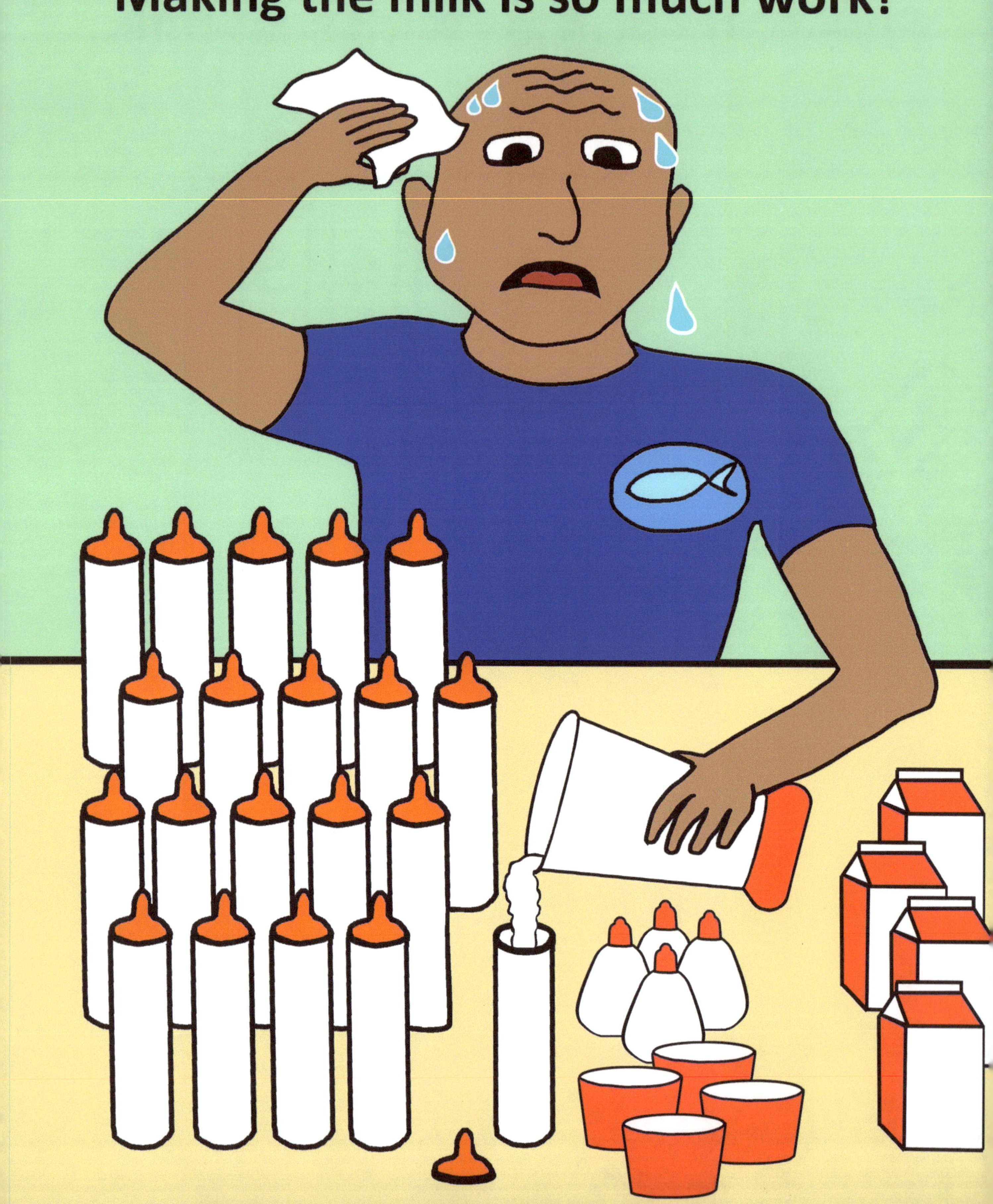

The team still has their usual work.

6:00 a.m.

The workday is very long.

8:00 p.m.

Then someone has a bright idea!

We can take
them home!

Aquarium staff and helpers volunteer to take the baby seals home.

One seal comes home with me.

It is my son PJ’s 10th birthday.

It is better than having
a birthday clown.

"Aww . . . I love the baby seal. I'll take care of it," said PJ's mom.

We have to clean up often

because the baby seal does not know how to use a toilet!

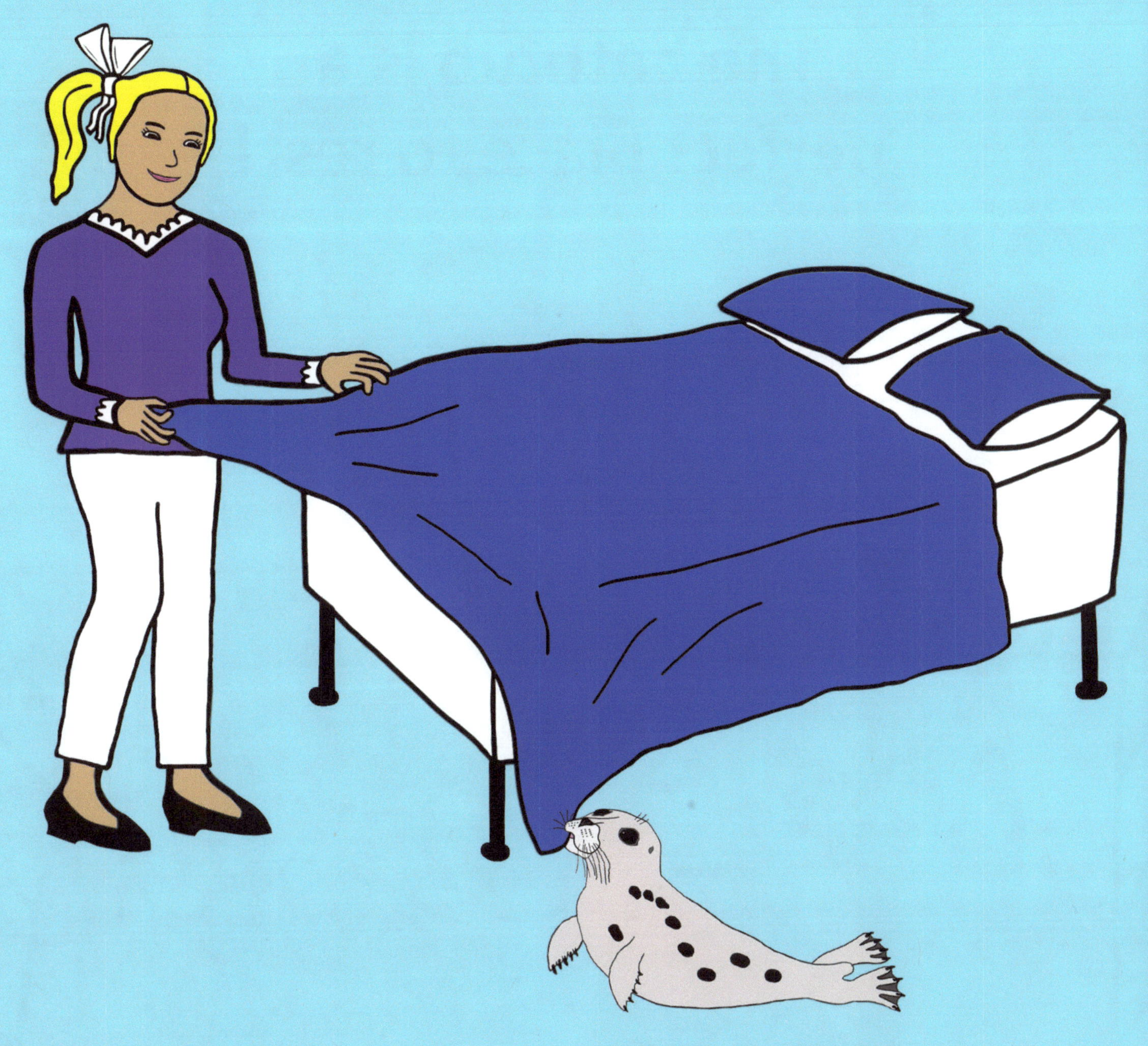

The baby seal helps
with the chores.

The bathtub is a perfect place to rest!

She can even swim in the kiddie pool outside!

She plays with our dog, Sheba.

We have a playdate at a tide pool with the other rescued seals.

Our seal grows bigger
and we give her a name.
My son, PJ, writes her a poem.

Cecil the seal,
came from the sea,
and lives with the Sieswerdas,
just like me.

by PJ Sieswerda,
10 years old

After five weeks,
Cecil starts to eat fish.

Once they are ready,
the rescued seals go
back to the sea.

But not Cecil.
She wants to stay with people.

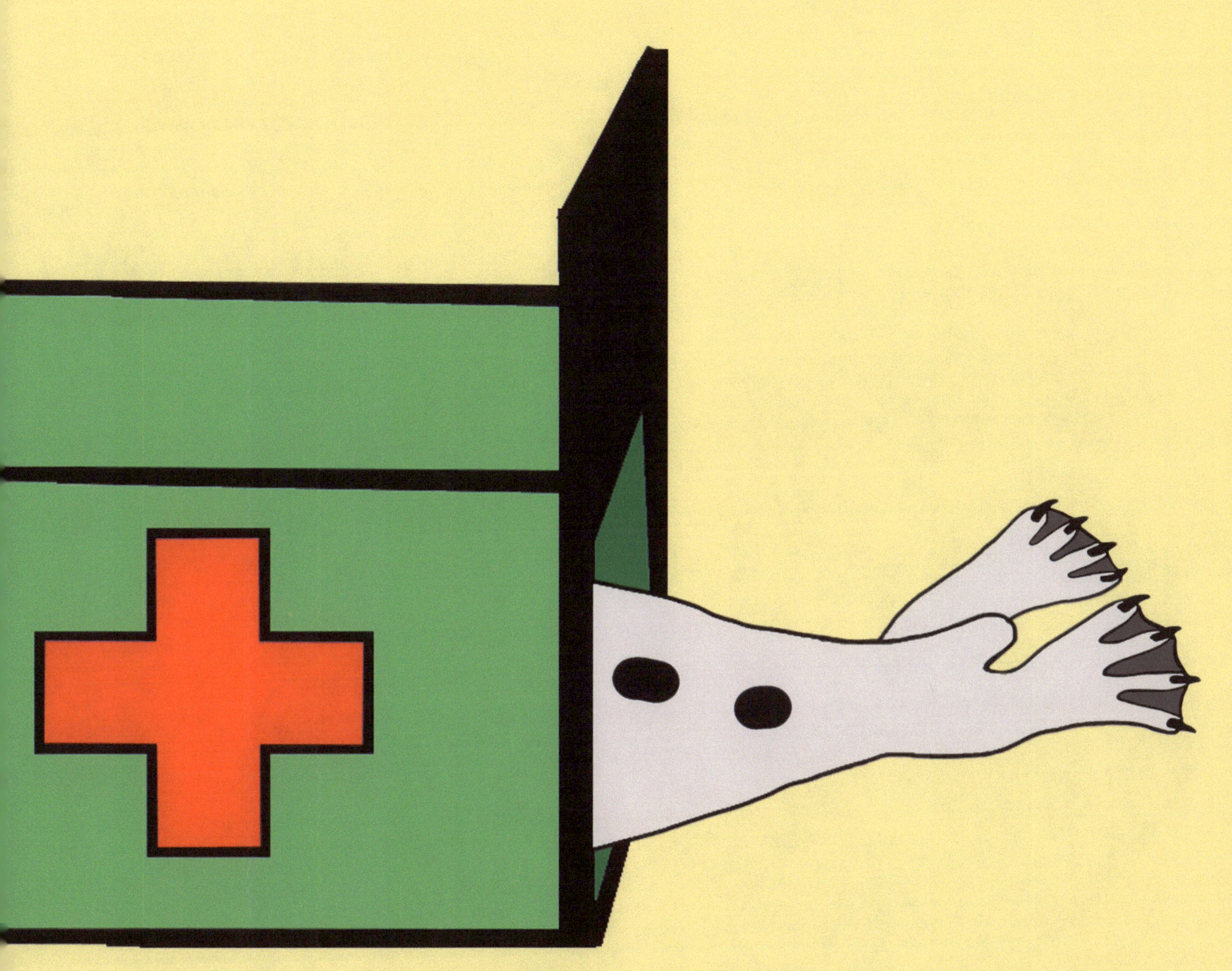

So Cecil goes back to the aquarium.

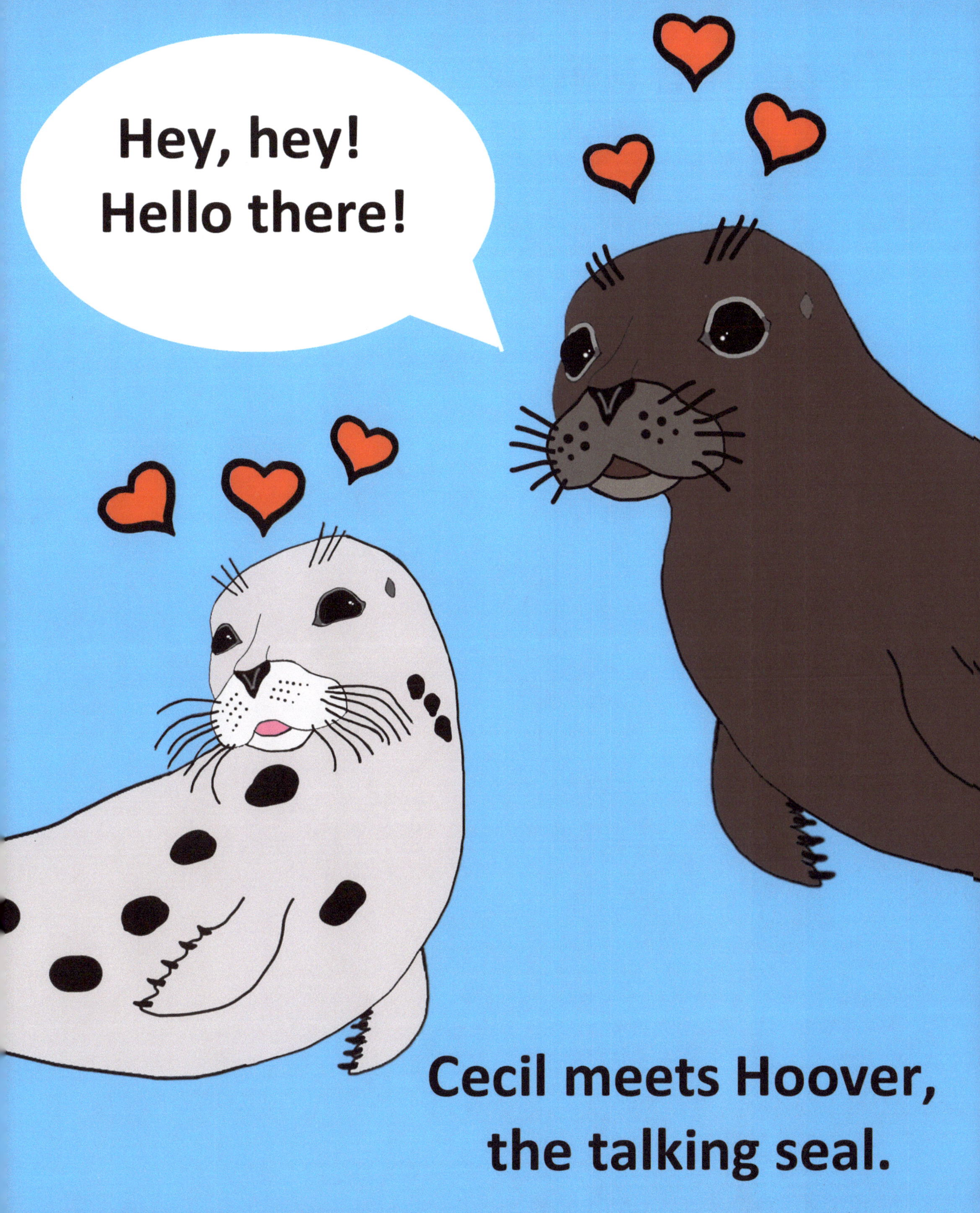
Hey, hey!
Hello there!
Cecil meets Hoover,
the talking seal.

Cecil and Hoover start a family. Their daughter is Trumpet, and their grandson is Chacoda.

Chacoda is trained to speak.

We can visit Cecil anytime!

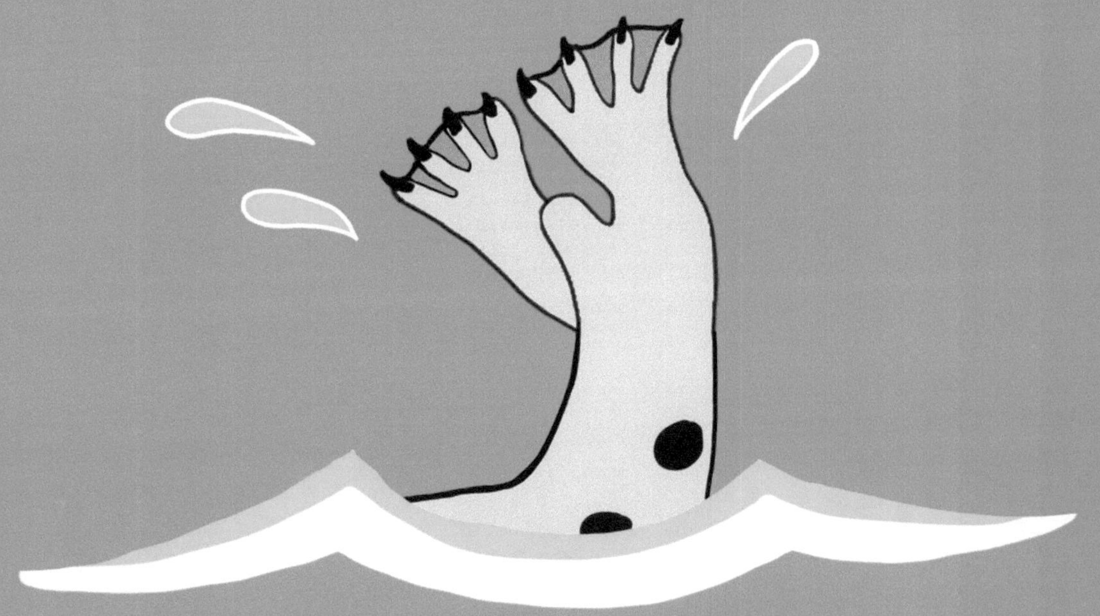

THE
END

Photo of Cecil in the bathtub in 1978 at
the Sieswerda family home in Massachusetts.

ACKNOWLEDGMENTS

Seal in the Bathtub has been waiting patiently, sitting beside the sink of imagination, for quite some time. Out of one small act of kindness—welcoming a seal into our world—many adventures have grown. This book could not have come to life without the inspiration, guidance, and love of several remarkable people, who continue to carry our story ever forward . . . toward brighter waters and generations yet to come.

To Paul L. Sieswerda, whose attitude of "anything can be done if you put your mind to it" was matched only by the steady support he built around him—he reminded us that bold ideas thrive when surrounded by teamwork.

To PJ Sieswerda, who has carried forward not only Paul L. Sieswerda's work, but his wonder. The stories that once lived in the family's memories have found new breath and meaning with his steadfast faith in the mission begun together.

To Joy Reidenberg, whose illustrations and deep knowledge of marine science gave this story its heartbeat. Her gifts brought the seal's world to life with both beauty and truth.

To Dorothy "Candi" Sieswerda, who showed through her motherly love that caring for a furry family member is no different than caring for each other. She taught us that, on this blue planet, we are all one family.

To Lorraine Fico-White and the Core Seal Team, with Lorraine's leadership shining through. They took command and proved that this mission could, and would, be completed.

To each parent and child, we offer our deepest gratitude. This book is as much yours as it is ours.

AUTHOR
Paul L. Sieswerda

Long before Paul L. Sieswerda became known for marine research, conservation, and public education, he was a man profoundly drawn to the sea itself. His journey began with seals—stranded pups brought into the New England Aquarium during the early days of marine mammal protection, long before public awareness had caught up. These animals sparked in him a sense of responsibility, compassion, and fascination that symbolized his belief that humans have a duty to care for the vulnerable creatures of the ocean.

This calling to the sea guided every chapter of his life. Whether he was helping rehabilitate marine mammals, guiding young aquarists, or building public exhibits that taught millions about ocean life, he carried with him a deep respect for the water and the beings who lived in it.

After retiring from a long and dedicated career as curator at both the New England Aquarium and the New York Aquarium, he continued his lifelong devotion. He founded Gotham Whale, a nonprofit grounded not just in research but in his enduring desire to share the wonder of marine life with future generations. His mission was never solely about whales. It was about connection: connection between humans and animals, between curiosity and stewardship, between a father and a son.

Sieswerda hoped that by opening people's eyes to the life just offshore—from seals to whales to the smallest creatures of the tide—he could inspire the same sense of awe and responsibility that guided him throughout his life. His legacy is not only in the science he contributed but in the moral compass he passed down: to respect the sea, to care for its creatures, and to leave the world better than we found it.

ILLUSTRATOR
Joy S. Reidenberg, PhD

Joy S. Reidenberg, PhD, is a professor at Icahn School of Medicine at Mount Sinai (in New York City), where she teaches medical and graduate students. She studies the comparative anatomy of animals adapted to environmental extremes, including pinnipeds (true seals, elephant seals, fur seals, sea lions, and walruses). Reidenberg has been featured in many international science and educational television documentaries, interviews, and TED talks. She is best known for her role as the comparative anatomist for *Inside Nature's Giants* (a TV documentary about large animal anatomy and evolution). Reidenberg is the scientific advisor for Gotham Whale, a citizen science nonprofit that tracks whales in New York. She loves to snorkel and scuba dive and relishes those rare moments when she has seen pinnipeds in their natural habitat. The above photo was taken on the coast of Vancouver Island, Canada, where a harbor seal came to rest on the nearby seaweed while Reidenberg was being filmed for a TV documentary about ocean animals.

CONTRIBUTING AUTHOR
Paul J. Sieswerda (PJ)

Paul J. Sieswerda (PJ) is the son and literary steward of Paul L. Sieswerda. Growing up, PJ was immersed early in the wonder of underwater exploration around the globe with his dad, from the vibrant reefs of the Bahamas and British Virgin Islands to the Red Sea, Micronesia, and Belize. It all started where his dad had volunteered at the New England Aquarium. Like father, like son, PJ's drive is to pass the same passion and curiosity from his father to his own three sons Canon, Emory, and Paul, so they, too, will carry forward the commitment to protect and celebrate our wonderful world of water!

OTHER BOOKS

by Paul L. Sieswerda and Joy S. Reidenberg

Big Whale, Big City

www.bestpub.com

BIG WHALE, BIG CITY is the story of a humpback whale named Jerry. His journey to New York City parallels the story of more and more humpbacks returning to the area in recent years. Jerry's adventure illustrates a whale's life history, how they feed, threats they face, and how the area around NYC is becoming a new feeding ground for humpbacks.

About Gotham Whale

www.GothamWhale.org

For over a decade, Gotham Whale has been dedicated to uncovering the magnificence and beauty of the whales that grace the waters of New York Harbor and beyond. Through the power of Citizen Science, we document their presence, study their behaviors, and share their incredible story with the world.

www.ingramcontent.com/pod-product-compliance
Lightning Source LLC
LaVergne TN
LVHW070223110826
845147LV00003B/628
9780941332453